Tongues in My Mouth

Poems by

Demetrice Anntía Worley

Main Street Rag Publishing Company
Charlotte, North Carolina

Cover art: © Rachel Eliza Griffiths
Author photo by: © Rachel Eliza Griffiths

Acknowledgments:

The following poems or versions of these poems have previously appeared in literary journals/anthologies:

Bread & Steel: Illinois Poets Reading Their Work: "Coming to Know Things"
Poet: "Indigo Blue"
Permafrost: "Ten Words Liberate a Life"
Rambunctious Review: "In Mother's House"
Reflections on a Gift of Watermelon Pickle and Other Modern Verse, 2ed: "Planting Shirt"
Reverie: "A Woman's Offering"
Risk, Courage, and Women: Contemporary Voices in Prose and Poetry: "Dancing in the Dark," "Judgment of Dissolution—A Found Poem," "No Position Is a Position"
Spirit and Flame: An Anthology of Contemporary African American Poetry: "Las Flores para una Nina Negra," "Tongues in My Mouth," "Dancing in the Dark"
Spoon River Poetry Review: "America Declares War on Girls"
Temba Tupu!/Walking Naked: Africana Women's Poetic Self-Portrait, "Tongues in My Mouth"
Women. Period.: "Blood Ritual"

Library of Congress Control Number: 2010940262

ISBN: 978-1-59948-283-5

Produced in the United States of America

Main Street Rag
PO Box 690100
Charlotte, NC 28227
www.MainStreetRag.com

In memory of my mother, Ernestine Randle Worley;
her words were a gift — any confusion is my own.

CONTENTS

4. TESTIFY

A CRITICAL VOICE: A FORWARD

Forewords for poetry collections can sometimes get in the way of the pleasures of discovery that often come from simply engaging a collection without the inevitable filter of a foreword. Of course, many who know this and are concerned about this, skip the foreword, and so I am clearly writing this for those of you who don't. Those like myself, who read forewords, should at least be assured that what I am attempting here is neither an academic appraisal of Demetrice Anntía Worley's elegant first collection of poems, "Tongues in My Mouth", nor is it an attempt to direct the reader on how he or she should encounter the work. I welcomed the chance to do this foreword because I have, in my cultural archive, a definition of the word "forward" that has less to do with the staid confines of Western academia and publishing, but with the dancehall of reggae culture. In the 1980s and 90s, a "forward" constituted a public expression of encouragement, affirmation, and a command to the artist to do what he or she does because by doing so the artist is advancing the cause of art, the cause of the dance, the cause of the struggle. So a crowd would shout, "Forward!" to an especially adept deejay or singer and that would be the greatest compliment ever. The word would become a noun, as in "yeah man, a nuff forward me get a de show," etc. So, what I do here is to champion Worley, celebrating the work she has managed to produce and offer her "nuff forwards" for this really important work. At the very least, you will know something of why I admire this work and why I am willing to stand in the crowd and shout, "Forward!"

Demetrice Anntía Worley's strengths as a poet are found in unexpected places for even as she is clearly a poet of witness, a poet committed to the task of truth-telling and political daring, it is in her craft, her impeccable poetic timing and her delicate management of sentiment and emotion that we witness her affecting powers as a poet. She is a meticulous craftsperson and she surprises us with the sharply drawn insights into human nature, even as she allows herself to admit to bewilderment at the inconstancy of human beings, including herself.

The poems in this book are united by a fascination with language—not for its linguistic possibilities alone, but for the very act of speaking, the very act of using words to fill empty spaces with meaning and confusion. In this sense, Worley's first book is about saying those things she has been longing to say for years. One has the sense that even as she seems intent on communicating with us with an audience, she is equally intent on, and satisfied with the empowerment inherent in the act of simply speaking to herself. Thus her poems are confessional in the strictest sense of that term. They confess, not to a confessor who will offer absolution, but they are confessions to the self, confessions that become public without leaving the viewer with the feeling of being a voyeur. She is not spilling her blood on the page—there is very little that could be deemed indulgent in these poems. Instead, she is using the poem to discover the truth inside of experience. She takes risks. Her greatest risk lies in her ability to say that she cannot confidently say that she understands everything she has seen, done, or heard, but to not let this silence her. Indeed, she is also saying that by writing these poems she may find her way to some meaning, even if the meaning lies only in that remarkable alchemy that poetry can be—that process of turning the mundane, the profane, the abject into something sublime, without ever diminishing the core of that thing. The metaphor is probably not correct. She is not changing anything, but discovering that which is inherent in the things she is seeing. When the blood from a woman's head, after she has been hit by her lover, is described as a beautiful flower blooming on a white tile, you know that beauty is not pretty, is not quaint, is not a deception—it is merely the inner value of a thing, even an ugly thing, that is shining through.

> My love,
> a red rose,
>   blooms
> on the white tiled floor.

Demetrice Anntía Worley

Violence, too, can be retrieved and managed by the act of retelling. Her blood on the white tile is like a blooming rose. Thus the violence becomes more alarming. The echo of Burns is not accidental, of course, but the startling violence is more pronounced by the juxtaposition of Robert Burns' not entirely un-melancholic lyric, "A Red, Red Rose". Worley's allusions to classical texts abound in the work, but she never does this to show off—indeed it is delicate handling of such moves that makes her work achieve the kind of layering that rewards constant rereading. In "Mourning Clothes" she puns somewhat obviously in the title and then invokes Shakespeare's Macbeth in the phrase "tomorrow's tomorrow":

> Tomorrow's tomorrow will find
> me in mourning clothes, white
> as our love, full as our hearts,
> when we last talked, making plans
> for lunch, coffee at the café,
> to right the world.

There is a delicate turning of suffering into beauty—it is the alchemy that makes the blues possible, or a song of lament into something close to sublime joy. But it is her mastery of craft that allows her to manage such fine tuned moves. It is how she turns the black of mourning clothes into something white; and the way she makes us ache when we think that she is talking about the loss of a friend who shared with her the fantasy of righting the world. Suddenly, her helplessness and the "un-rightness" of death weigh heavily on us. And yet, there is no other way to describe this deft management of grief but as something beautiful.

Worley is a poet of witness. She writes like one who has spent time obsessing about the ideas that have caused her concern and pain, and she has finally had the chance to shape those thoughts and obsessions into music. Her poems are engaged in the way that citizen poets engage with the social and political realities surrounding them. But it is hard to find an agenda here other than the compelling art of truth telling. And this is why her poems can shift with complete ease from the consideration of the fate of Assata Shakur, a political prisoner in the American system, to her mother's callous disregard for the suicide of her own daughter. What makes these subjects part of the same impulse for Worley is the fact that they dare to expose the shock or inhumanity in those whose callous disregard for the suffering cause them to speak painful things about the victim. Her dead sister has no voice, and Worley dares to upend the notion of a mother's pure sentiment for her offspring—and she does this with the same commitment as she does the notion of a politically just system in American society. Someone is lying, and she won't allow the lie to stand.

In "Promises", and in the poems from the section, "Outline" we see the delineation of the hurts that shape a woman's identity. In "Promises" hurt is an understatement—a white doctor who molests a girl and a man who comes by her home and does the same. There are no answers, no way to process into rage the confusion of a five year old. All she can do is run. It is Worley's skill that allows the subtlest of cracks that becomes a chasm of pain: "I closed my eyes. It hurt to be me." One has the sense that this is both the voice of the girl and perhaps even more, the voice of the woman who was the girl.

Worley finds poems in the luminal moments of life—places where things change. Her poem, "Judgment of Dissolution—A Found Poem", about divorce, for instance, takes the dry legal language and manages to create a subtext that is filled with the pain and disappointment of divorce. Somehow, the lack of children in the marriage is a metaphor for a great deal that has been sterile/barren in the marriage. In italics, the commentary is stark:

> One spring I dreamt babies,
> playing on my lap, tugging
> at my hair, sleeping in my arms.
> He was not ready.
>
> Four years later he pleaded,
> I refused to respond.

Demetrice Anntía Worley

The subtitle, "A Found Poem" is almost a misnomer for Worley since there is a real sense in which all her poems are "found poems". She salvages these beautifully formed pieces from the details of her life and her encounters with the world whether she is meditating on the idea of being alone, the shadow of divorce and separation palpable in the space she occupies in the poem "Building Fires", or her time reflecting on the meaning of invisibility and femininity in her poems set in Cairo ("An African American Woman's Offering: A Bop"). And even when she is being unabashedly political and protesting at full throttle, she remains fully whole, fully present emotionally. Note, in the harrowing poem "America Declares War on Girls", the way the moan of the poet as she watches the news and finds herself transported to the scenes of so many brutish crimes against girls, becomes the moan of the girl at the end of the poem—a moan that is eventually silenced:

He pulls her white cotton panties
below her knees, jabs a stick into her vagina.
She moans. He stuffs yellow/brown leaves
in her mouth, stops her voice, her cries, her breath.

This silencing, this press towards voiceless-ness is at the heart of these poems. And so we gradually come to recognize the sophistication of her sectional-titles ("Articulate", "Vocalize", "Outline", and "Testify") and, more importantly, of her collection's title, "Tongues in My Mouth", where the entire book becomes a contemplation on the meaning of voice—the meaning of saying on so many levels. Here, it is the woman's voice that seeks to say what must be said, and importantly, Worley recognizes that there are many voices richly gathered in her mouth. The poems push back against the tyranny of silence.

It is common practice now to try to underplay any suggestion that the "I" in a poem is even remotely related to the poet. We speak of the "speaker" and the "persona", working hard to create a distance between the poet and the voice in the poem. Of course, it is an act of presumptive politeness on our part, an act that seeks to not presume too much of the poet, and that seems to want to allow the poet the freedom to be as inventive as possible without the tyranny of assumptions about autobiography. The downside to this, of course, is that it shares much with some deconstructionists who would argue the death of the author. An absurd idea for poetry, but one that still holds sway in some quarters. I fear, though, that we often, in the process, lose sight of the sheer courage and risk that a poet undertakes to tackle certain subjects and to, in the process, reveal herself. While I have not attempted to align Worley's biography with the details in her poems, I venture to say that she is of the view that all poetry that we write is, at some level, autobiographical in all the ways that autobiography, though slippery and unreliable, is ultimately personal.

I leave this collection feeling as if I have been in the presence of a woman called Demetrice Anntía Worley, a poet who has learned to take the detritus of life and turn them into powerful and moving statements about self and about community. She has seen hard things, she has lost loves, she has flirted with the outrageous and the taboo, and she has come out of all of this with the grace that comes from making wonderful art. If, like me, you are as much drawn to the narrative of our daily lives with their mundane happenings and dramas alike, as you are to the brilliance of well-developed craft and the practice of elegant verse writing, then you will find much to enjoy in this collection of poems that do not shy away from tough political questions and troubling emotional and psychological issues.

For you to echo my "forward" of affirmation and praise for this collection, you will have to read these poems, and come to your own conclusions about their power and force. My expectation is that you will join me in shouting "forward!" when you are through.

Kwame Dawes
Columbia, SC

Your silence will not protect you.
— Audre Lorde

1. ARTICULATE

COMING TO KNOW THINGS

i.

Michelle, at fourteen you knew things
I couldn't understand, like FM radio
waves rolling across your new stereo,
a fuller sound than my tinny AM transistor.
Nearly every FM station sounded like
nasal tones, "Public Radio," except
the ones playing hard guitar twangs
I'd never heard on Chicago's WVON,
"Voice of the Negro."

ii.

Michelle, at fourteen we listened to songs
pressed into black vinyl, LP albums you bought
for *the amazing price of eleven cents, a penny
per platter*. White bands I didn't know like
Clear Water Revival, Steely Dan, and
Bachman Turner Overdrive made you dance
across your stepmother's glossy hardwood floors.

When you read the record club's
collection letter, you laughed, explained
how you didn't use your own name
on the order slip; told me even Perry Mason
couldn't convince a jury that a black girl
living on Chicago's west side would listen
to Lynard Skynard. I believed you
when you said, "I didn't commit a crime."

iii.

Michelle, at fourteen we kissed,
said we were friends for life. I wanted
you to soothe me with kisses like those
you shared with Eric; he filled you
with more than my wonderment.
The girls called you "nasty."
I/he/we knew milk breath sweetness,
silky sweat, black feathered line
from navel to pubes.

Demetrice Anntía Worley

BUILDING FIRES

Inside my husband's log cabin,
bundled in a blanket,
hands in mittens,
I wander
room to room.
Heard him say,
"Don't forget the fire."

> *Across the dead end road,*
> *chimney smoke blankets*
> *neighbors' white roofs.*

Transplanted
from Chicago Westside,
I survive black nights
in Burlington County
with tepid milk.
Mornings, at four o'clock,
I scribble with black
and peacock blue ink,
on yellow tablets.
Thin pages.

> *Snow drifts against*
> *the sliding glass door.*
> *The wood stove stays cold.*

I survive daylight
watching soap operas,
flat images,
filling hours,
remembering days
in the city

occupied
with things.

Northeast wind blows
snow, corn stalk stubble
against the windows.

A sack of ice,
I sink into the couch,
imagine placing kindling
on spent ash,
laying oak crisscross
against itself,
crushing manuscript
pages into balls
filling empty spaces,
striking a wooden match.

Hear myself,
"Start a fire today."

Demetrice Anntía Worley

A WRITER'S BEGINNINGS

My first fiction—*We don't have any food; I'm
hungry.* I don't breathe. I don't sweat. I stare.
Mrs. Moore's green eyes flick across my face.
I couldn't say fourth-grade-failed spelling test
remained unsigned. Chalk calloused fingers pinch
my ashy tan arm, lead me to the closed
lunchroom. Under a white woman's pale eyes,
choking on dry crusty bread and peanut
butter, I eat, again. My first lunch, I
ate at home, reoccurring pinto beans
and rice, under my mother's tired brown eyes.

School officials report my nine-year-old
tale. My mother's fist nestles in my cheek;
dry-eyed, I accept her exquisite rage.

MY EYES BETRAY ME

i.

His mouth opens,
the lesson begins.
My lover's accented
words rush past my ears,
ghost flapping, *Your eyes,*
betray you. Brown eyes
are the color of bullshit.
Hahaha. His laughter
draws me in.

ii.

The mirror above the dresser holds
his pale naked bathroom reflection,
head thrown back, mouth slack,
the taste of me mingles
with minty freshness.
A little slides down his throat.
He coughs, spits me,
the tingle in his mouth,
into the toilet.

Demetrice Anntía Worley

iii.

Shut up, woman!
I close my mouth.
Remember lover's
Puerto Rican songs.
My head thuds
against the door frame,
mini-starbursts explode.
Words rush past my ears:
ghosts dance in my mind,
flapping gossamers pirouette,
spinning on and on
        and stop.

iv.

My love,
a red rose,
    blooms
on the white tiled floor.

A LOVE POEM

i.

What if my decadence
is me without politeness,
the pretense of prudishness,
the falseness of pretending,
is me loving with a heart beating
within a warmness, is me
loving with fingertips aching
to trace a curve's softness,
is me loving with a tongue longing
to roll over the fullness of your taste,
is me loving with eyes seeing
color in blackness, is me
loving/seeing the realness of me?

ii.

What if I shared my heart,
opened it up, exposed
raw, warm, pulsing
veins carrying
me through me,
exposed
the vulnerable spot,
and you
put a finger
on it and stopped
the beating of my heart?

Demetrice Anntía Worley

MOURNING CLOTHES

Today I wore mourning clothes,
turtleneck, jacket, slacks, black
as my grief, flat as my eyes.
Tomorrow will find the same
color draping my silent body,
a cushion between me
and a darkness whose bottom
will not sound when I land.

Today your daughter's whispered
words, *My mother was right
with me, my sister, God*,
filled my empty pew,
filled the church,
a cool balm,
a laying on of hands.

Tomorrow's tomorrow will find
me in mourning clothes, white
as our love, full as our hearts,
when we last talked, making plans
for lunch, coffee at the café,
to right the world.

MISERIES

If, like the old people say, misery comes in threes—
 A black man, a father,
 an Extreme Ryder,
 in his Band of Bruthaz,
 a Majestic Spade, leans
 into the Route 29 corner,
 90 miles per hour, polishing
 against asphalt, splitting
 helmet in half—
my cousin Tehran's death was first.

If, like the old people say, misery comes in threes—
 London's Underground
 Russell Station platform,
 mice dart over gray
 dust covered ties
 avoiding charged rail.
 I inhale sooty air, coat
 pink lung tissue with industrial age.
 Heart beats. I marvel at my calmness,
 standing 500 ft underground,
 before announcer's clipped
 "The Brixton train is delayed
 Due to a death on the tracks"—
London tube carriages exploding was second.

If, like the old people say, misery comes in threes—
 Daily, my man and I discuss headlines,
 New York Times, CNN, Daily Drudge,
 The Defender, The Final Call, *burning*
 through day and anytime minutes. Two months
 ago, he asked me to marry him. Today,
 he says, "We need to talk"—
my fiancé's halting silence was third.

FULL OF GRACE

In a dream
I am on my knees
armed with strong,
clear plastic tape,
frantically mending
a rip in the carpet,
a small piece is missing.

Another woman bends,
reaches for a corner.
No, I scream
Don't lift it up.
The woman ignores me.

Under the carpet,
the hole is larger
than last time.
Gray mist floats
from the blackness.
Fear rises
in my stomach.

With open hands,
I try to push down
the darkness. Mist gnarls
itself in my hair, pulls
me into the hole. Falling,
I pray, *Hail Mary,*
full of grace. The Lord
is with thee. Blessed
art thou amongst women,
and blessed is the fruit
of thy womb . . . .

Tepid blood slides
down my thighs,
a sacramental offering,
I cross myself.

In the night sky
the full moon shines
in solitary confinement.

Demetrice Anntía Worley

LONDON UNDERGROUND FROM RUSSELL SQUARE TO BRIXTON — A FOUND POEM

Russell Square   Underground
Entry   Next Lift
125 Steps   to Platform
Mind   *the gap*

Piccadilly Line   *This Train*
terminates in   *Uxbridge*
Obstructing   the Doors
Can Be   Dangerous

The next   *stop is Holborn*
Covent Garden   *Leicester Square*
Piccadilly   *Circus*
Green Park   way out

Busking   is Prohibited
Penalty   £200
Why Aren't   You Holding
onto the Rail?   Victoria Line

This train   *terminates in Brixton*
Obstruct~~ing~~   the Door
~~Can~~ Be   Dangerous
The next stop   *is Victoria*

Pimlico   *Vauxhall*
Mind the gap   way out
Entry Denied   Seek Assistance
Exit Brixton   Underground

TERRA FIRMA

Wal-Mart plastic bags in hand, I fumble
for car keys; out the corner of my eye
I'm watching two white teenaged boys

in camouflage green, looking at me sideways.
They see a brown-skinned-afro-wearing woman,
searching frantically in her purse; they laugh,

jump into their rusty F-250 pick-up,
slam the doors—a rifle rests in its rack.
I look up from my purse, an audible *oh* slips

from my parted lips as pristine altocumulus clouds
streak across the azure troposphere. I sway—
> *This surreal sky is a fast forward scene*
> *flashing on an Imax cinema's*
> *72 foot wide screen—rounded edges*
> *on the periphery hold buildings*

> *erect as clouds speed*
> *across the sky, sun climbing,*
> *moving east to west, descending,*

> *blue shifting, twilight, darkness—*
> *except I'm on terra firma,*
> *affixed to the planet's axis,*

> *feeling the planet hurl itself*
> *through space; in this nanosecond*
> *I'm anchored to the Earth's core,*

> *connected to mass, energy, larger*
> *than young, laughing white supremacists.*
The moment passes. I blink; close my lips.

Demetrice Anntía Worley

Keys in hand I let myself into the car.
Near the parking lot exit, the tires'
asphalt squeal mixes with adolescent guffaws.

Sighing, I glance through the windshield. Two
gray-white seagulls circle overhead, dancing
on the wind, far from the water that feeds them.

VISUAL MARKERS

The purpose [of the control unit] is to control revolutionary
attitudes in the prison system and in society at large.

i.

Our representatives state,
"We have no political prisoners
in the U.S.," but I can't forget
the documentary's images—
three women held
in the Lexington, Kentucky,
federal prison control unit
surrounded by no windows,
white walls, white floors,
continuous white lights.
Dressed in shapeless blue smocks,
these women counted 24-hour days.
Whiteness is a form
of psychological torture,
it leaves no visual marks.

ii.

Prisons are for prisoners;
holding places, isolation camps
for those who refuse
to follow the rules
like three women serving
a combined 140 years
in the Lexington Control Unit.
The FBI had visual evidence,
Alejandrina Torres on videotape
building a bomb. They accused

Demetrice Anntía Worley

her of wanting to blow-up
buildings; she said
she was protesting
U.S. colonial domination
of Puerto Rico. The FBI
had visual evidence,
Susan Rosenberg's fingerprints
on explosives and weapons;

she said she was protesting
North America's imperialism.
She was given 58 years—
the longest sentence in U.S.
history for weapons possession.
The third woman, Silvia Baraldini,
was sentenced 40 years
for "racketeering"—aiding,
in Assata Shakur's
1979 prison escape.
The FBI had visual evidence,
her words, written
to express her support
for the Black and Puerto Rican
Liberation Movements,
mono- and poly-,
no tri-, syllabic symbols,
signs of identification,
small words placed next
to one another, a train of thought
derailed before pulling
into the station.

iii.

Last night I dreamt
I was in a courthouse trying
to escape. I kept opening doors,
saw rooms filled with empty faced
white men sitting in rows,
listening to a hooded man read
my alleged crimes from a black book.
The pages were blank. In the hall
white men gestured with line-less palms
for me to follow them. The floor
changed into water. I couldn't swim.
Reached for their hands, I couldn't
get a grip. Remembered it was air
I was breathing, found myself
on the courthouse steps.
An old Black woman, dressed
in a long, patch-worked dress,
nodded at me, pointed to the sign
above the courthouse doors:
             Black Ink
                on
          White Paper
I woke up.
The after image
left no marks.

Demetrice Anntía Worley

WITHOUT HEARING A QUESTION, MY MOTHER ANSWERS

We've never had good luck with those people,
Her arthritic calcified fingers hover
above vine ripened Kentucky Wonder beans,
finding a blemish free one, she feels

it weakness, snaps it in half.
*You remember what happened
to your cousin Lillian?* I shift
on the porch swing. *He came here*

without a dime in his pockets. My mother's
quick fingers snap another bean. *You can't trust
a green suited man. Nobody paid him any mind,
except Lillian. Three weeks later she ran*

off with him to Detroit. On Hobart Street,
the fire station's siren begins to serenade
volunteers. Its call wraps around
my head, tightening,

until its high pitch whine becomes a wail,
a mother's cry for a daughter who has
left town. *No forwarding address.
Only a post card from Detroit.*

*You remember what happened to your cousin
Lillian, don't you?* The siren gradually *aaahs*
into the humid afternoon air, its grip lessens
across my temples. I look across the dirt packed

yard, over my car, down the street,
across the interstate, into my lover's
hazel eyes, into a restless sea.
My mother stands, rests a stainless

steel bowl full of Kentucky Wonders
on her hip. *He threw her fool ass*
out of a fourth-story window.
The screen door slaps shut.

My thin caramel fingers, shadows
of my mother's, clumsily pick-up
a bean, tear it. Ragged pieces fall
into a half-empty bowl.

TONGUES IN MY MOUTH

Behold, I open my mouth;
the tongue in my mouth speaks.
　　—King James Bible,
　　　English Standard Edition, Job 33:2

Tired of waiting for me,
my ancestor's spirits are lifting
my heavy tongue, forming
words in my mouth.

Tuwa wasteicillia maka kin lecela
tehan yunkelo, my paternal
great-great grandmother's Sioux voice,
guides me beyond concern for self.

Sa koon ain je gun, my maternal
great-great grandmother's Blackfeet voice,
the light of her soul, locates my words
Ewúro ò fi tojo korò, my foremothers'
Yoruba voices tell me, *listen,*
hear the wisdom.

My ancestors are making me
practice my languages,
forcing me to make foreign sounds,
to turn new words over,
until the tongues in my mouth
speak in a single voice,
until the tongues in my mouth,
speak the truth that no one wants to hear.

2. VOCALIZE

FEMICIDE/*FEMICIDIO* ~ THE MURDERED AND DISAPPEARED WOMEN OF *CIUDAD JUÁREZ*, MÉXICO

*Amnesty International has confirmed that since 1992
the number of murdered women and girls from and around
Ciudad Juárez is 475, and it believes over 5,000 women and
girls have disappeared.*
— Barbara Martinez Jittner, Independent Film Maker

i.

On this eve of the dead, I cry out loud,
"*por favor Virgen de Guadalupe*, don't
forsake me," before I open the door,
before I see e*l policía* flat
black eyes, before his mouth opens to tell
me, my Solana, *m'hija*, is dead.

Our women and girls are vanishing from
Ciudad Juárez. Mi casa. All he brings
is a box with two leg bones; "Proof," he says.
¡Ha! I've seen death; I know bones.
I cross myself, speak a *mamá's* clear truth:
    "On *m'hija's* First Holy Communion,
     She broke her right leg in two places.
     These bones, two left leg bones, are not Solana's."

ii.

"These bones, two left leg bones, are not Solana's."
mamá says, before closing the door. She passes
my bedroom. I am here, but we did not
have my party, *mi quinceañera.*
I'm fifteen today, a woman.

Alva, *mi*
amiga, heard yesterday that a girl
from *Colonia Paz,* never came home from her job.
Twice a day, I pray, *Virgen de Guadalupe*
save me from factory work in *Ciudad Juárez;*

Two weeks in this silent room, watching Pretty
Boy, parakeet of *mi hermana,* pace his perch. The last
three days his water cup has remained full.
Today, I found him on the cage floor.
Today, I stopped waiting for Solana.

iii.

Today, I stopped waiting for Solana
to appear at the bus stop *de la maquila.*
For two weeks,
                    I've waited for her smile.
At our work stations, *las chicas* and I whisper
the names of *la muerta* between thin lips.
We sew capris, daily quotas for a big store
across *la frontera.*
                    We asked the Bosses
for parking lot lights, guard posts. They gave us
whistles, self-defense talks.
                    We asked *los policías*
to protect us; they do not listen. *El Diablo*
and *los policías,* one and the same.

Las chicas y yo work in silences.
We need our jobs. We have *familias.*
The Bosses say, "Women can be replaced."

iv.

Bosses Say, Women Can Be Replaced—
AP Wire. NAFTA's enactment
has allowed foreign-owned factories
to cash in on low-cost labor, easy access
to U.S. markets. But at *maquiladoras,*
assembly plants, women bank no bargains;
their week lasts sixty to seventy hours;
wages $5.75 a day *[milk costs $2.50*
a gallon]; pregnant women are denied jobs
or fired; workers are attacked for drawing
attention to callous working conditions.
After shift changes gates are locked, and workers
turned away if three minutes late. Forced
to return home alone, often in the dark.

v.

I return home, alone, to darkness and
silence, after reconstructing remains
of Juarez's unidentified dead
women. Every night my home, like the white,
sterile Chihuahua State Forensic morgue,
fills with bodies, parts: acid etched skin; breasts,
slashed, stabbed, gnawed; raped vaginas; heads leaking
from gunshot wounds. These girls have long hair, brown
complexions. They are young. Someone's child.
My child. She lived for seventeen years in this house.
If Paloma's case, *caso de m'hija*
isn't solved, I'll join other mothers, plant pink/
black crosses outside state police offices. Our
united voices speak louder than one tongue.

vi.

United voices speak louder than one tongue;
we paint black and pink crosses, march the streets
saying names of three hundred and twenty *niñas*
y mujeres raped, mutilated, *matadas*—
"Laura Ramos Monarrez, Lourdes Lucero
Campos, Sagrario Gonzalez Flores,
Paloma Villa Rodriguez, Guadalupe
Estrada Salas, Solana Sanchez Cruz . . ."
our *hijas y hermanas*.
                                    Las policías
say *prostitutes, mujeres del fugitivos*:
we know *el secreto* pile of bones; missing
files; a woman's body clothed in another
woman's dress; *evidencia destruida*—
five hundred kilos of clothing burned last week.

vii.

I boxed a hundred pounds of clothing today;
cleared closets of capris, tee-shirts; threw
away Halloween bag of Brach's candy corn;
a label funeral for *Made in Mexico*.
My protest, against NAFTA, the Mexican
Government, the Juárez police, makes me
a world citizen; makes me read today's newspaper:
"Six Peoria Black Women Murdered, Bodies
Found Over Last Three Years in Rural Countryside."
I read their names: Brenda Erving, Frederickia Brown,
Linda Neal, Barbara Williams, Sabrina Payne, Wanda

Jackson. Paper says "prostitutes, addicts." Turn page,

"Four Peoria Black Women Still Missing."
On this eve of the dead, I cry out, loud.

3. OUTLINE

PROMISES

The car stopped close to my fence.
He said I was pretty—me, a brown girl,
thick braids, wide smile, ashy knees.
He said we would be gone for just

a little while. He promised not to hurt
me. But like the white doctor who told me
it was a special way to take my pulse,
he slid his fingers into moist places.

I closed my eyes. It hurt to be me.
No air. I couldn't breathe.
Sitting next to myself, I dreamed
of snowflakes covering the streets.

Weeks later, when I learned to tie
droopy shoelaces, my parents bought promised
red P. F. Flyers. I ran faster, jumped
higher than any five-year-old girl on my block.

MILK TEETH

My father said baby teeth
fall out. I waited. Tried wiggling
them. No pain. They shifted,
a slight resistance.

Milk-teeth pushed forward,
permanents inpatient
to take their rightful place.
Old and new together,
two short rows. I waited.

I stopped smiling, talking.
Refused to open my mouth
except to eat. They stayed.
I waited. My father said.
"It will happen."

I remember riding one bus,
transferring to the el train,
walking for blocks.
My father said nothing
the entire time. At seven-years-old,
I knew this visit was going to cost
"too much money."

In a white office, the dentist looked
in my mouth, asked my father, *Why did
you wait so long?* My father answered,
"She wouldn't let them go."

Demetrice Anntía Worley

COLORED GIRL

In 1968 when Martin Luther King Jr., died
I stopped being colored.

> *Sitting cross-legged,*
> *on avocado shag carpet, I stare*
> *expressionless at our nineteen inch*
> *black and white television —*
> *Samantha Stevens rides her broom*
> *side-saddle across* Bewitched's
> *opening credits. Newsbreak:*
> *Walter Cronkite's pale eyes*
> *do not blink as he informs*
> *the nation,* Negroes are rioting,
> on Chicago's west side, in Harlem,
> Watts. *Across our Zenith's screen,*
> *light and dark gray images shift,*
> *people running, buildings burning,*
> *a colored man, carrying a naked*
> *white mannequin, raises his fist,*
> *cries,* Power to the people.

I wondered about darkness as only
an eight-year-old child can wonder —

> *That April evening, standing*
> *in my parents' bedroom,*
> *forehead pressed against*
> *the cool window pane,*
> *I watch the orange glow*
> *from the riot's flames, radiate*
> *on the Chicago horizon*

when would blackness envelop
my caramel-colored skin.

AGAINST THE WALL

i.

Hundreds of well-dressed art patrons talk,
laugh and eat in a hotel ballroom. I wear
a lime-green polyester dress, slick pressed
hair, all of thirteen-years-old. Chewing
in small, proper bites, I make my father,
mother, brothers, and grandmother proud;
they watch me through the ballroom door's
narrow windows. Their mouths,
black ovals, hang open.

After I receive my writing award,
a concerned white woman asks,
"What do you want to be when you
grow up?" I look across tables of seated
people. Standing in the rear of the room,
their backs against the wall, my family
is smiling. I open my mouth to speak,
form a round, dark place, no words.

ii.

When I was in college,
I took a black woman friend
to the *Rocky Horror Picture Show*.
As rolls of toilet tissue, water,
and burnt toast showered on us,
the white audience sang,
"Let's do the time warp again."
She asked if I treated all my friends
this way. My mouth fell open, no sounds.

Demetrice Anntía Worley

TEN WORDS LIBERATE A LIFE

Three weeks into my slow, starving death, I
feign sleep; listen to white noise, feel its flat

warmth blanket my ninety-five pounds. My eyes
open, focus on my door-framed mother

blocking light. A yellow aura halos
her head. Her brown eyes flash a fury I've

never seen in my seventeen years. It's
a blinding vortex gaining speed, spinning;

a raging snow blizzard in a glass dome.
Her mouth opens. Keen, acute sound transcends

white noise: *Whether you're here or not, the sun
will rise tomorrow.* She closes her mouth,

returns to bed. I shake. The blankets are
too thin. Frigid air stiffens my joints, bones.

IN MOTHER'S HOUSE

every Thursday
I am two dimensional,
thin enough
to walk down her hall
cluttered with small, still
figurines,
birds in flight,
clowns tossing hoops
poised in mid-air.

I sit on the edge
of plastic couch covers,
protection from small
grape-jelly-covered fingers,
and stare
at faded gold brocade.

We exchange polite
conversation
before she asks why,
after 24 years,
am I still in school.
I answer her question
and my words,
paisley petals,
drift into my lap.

Thursdays
I leave,
avoiding staring
into her.
Behind me,
the doorknob turns.
I exhale
and draw in fresh air.

Demetrice Anntía Worley

FREE FALLING

In this dream
darkness swallows me—
I'm free falling in an abyss.

My dry eyes are open.
No images of nursing
at my mother's breast,
playing tag in the street,
or praying on a 1968
Dodge Polara's back seat
under the pulsing weight
of a fullback comfort me.

My dry eyes are open,
I tumble inside
velvet blackness,
a white-out
in black face.
Performing a ballet,
I gracefully,
twist and turn.
Whooshing air
caresses fine hairs
on my arms/face.

Final impact
is not frightening—
This time
my dry eyes are open.

BLOOD RITUAL

Humid air swaddles my hot body.
With one bare leg draped over
the back of the porch swing,

I slowly sway in rural blue-black darkness.
Close-bitten nails. Chipped red polish.
Fingers folded flat against belly, I count

28 days since the last full moon.
On the eastern horizon,
a billowy thunderhead,

thousands of feet high, expansive
as the distance between *quicken*
and *termination*, stations itself.

Pulsating yellow-pink, and purple flashes
illuminate the gray-white cloud,
transient brilliancy.

A white flash quivers
through it. My skin tingles.
I listen for a thunderous rumble

to determine the lightning's
closeness: *One thousand one,*
one thousand two, the swing stops.

My moist hands press down on my womb.
I inhale heavy ionized air, smell
dewy soil's pungent iron odor.

INDIGO BUNTING

The aftermath of a week of planning
is a hole covered with dirt and flowers
from his daughter, grandchildren,
brother, and sister. We step around
the marker, flush with the close,
cropped grass. The sun beats down
on our heads as we walk
to the older section.

We pause in a granite angel's shade.
Her hands reach toward the sky.
I attempt to tell you about
the Indigo Bunting fluttering
on the periphery of my vision.
It's a blue so intense,
I can taste it, like anesthesia
rising from my lungs,
a sweetness in my nostrils.
Dancing across my vocal cords,
it becomes moths' wings, dusty,
beating against the roof of my mouth.

You wait. I can't repeat the words.
They float through the angel's fingers.

JUDGMENT OF DISSOLUTION—
A FOUND POEM

Now comes the Plaintiff, 32 years of age,
employed outside the home.
I manage other people's lives,
carefully penciled appointments.

The Defendant is 34 years of age,
employed outside the home.
He manages other people's money,
investing for their futures.

The Plaintiff and Defendant
were lawfully married
in this state, and said marriage
was duly registered in this county.

The parties lived together
after their marriage,
a total of 3,480 days,
10 hours, 28 minutes,

but have ceased to live together
as husband and wife,
or as lovers, or as friends,
and now reside in separate dwellings.

The wife of the marriage
is not now pregnant; there are
no living children of the marriage,
whether born or adopted.

Demetrice Anntía Worley

One spring I dreamt babies,
playing on my lap, tugging
at my hair, sleeping in my arms.
He was not ready.

Four years later he pleaded,
I refused to respond.
Irreconcilable differences
between the parties have caused

the irreparable breakdown
of the marriage. Efforts
at reconciliation have failed,
silent dinners, empty kisses,

nothing is different from the way
it was yesterday or the day
before or the day before,
and further attempts at reconciliation

would be impracticable. Wherefore,
the Plaintiff respectively prays for
and seeks the following relief:
a judgment of Dissolution of Marriage

be awarded to the parties,
and the Plaintiff's maiden name,
my birth name, my current name,
is the name the Plaintiff wishes to remain.

PLANTING SHIRT

A blue cotton smock hangs in my closet. In this smock
my cousin Lois planted tomatoes and collard greens
beside her garage. Called it her planting shirt. Told

me, *When I plant my seedlings with this shirt on, I don't
lose the young ones.*
                    Once I saw her look up from
placing thin, stringy roots in the dirt, and the faded,
blue smock made the gray in her brown eyes flutter.

I told her she only wore it to make the plants take pity
on her. Now, I wear the shirt. I remember Lois'
seedlings, and I plant my sorrow deep.

Demetrice Anntía Worley

WHEN I SPOKE ABOUT THE FOG, YOU THOUGHT I MEANT THE WEATHER

St. Mary's twin cathedral spires float
like islands in the December fog
hanging over downtown.
In the restaurant
the waitress gives us a table
with a view—two seagulls glide,
dip, languidly flap their wings,
in front of our window,
a white backdrop highlights
their dance, below, the cold
dark gray Illinois River slaps
the eroding red bricks; white mist
blankets the smooth-stoned shore—
you tell me, *The weather girl
is always wrong*, look back
at your menu. I stare
at your dirty fingernails.

LAS FLORES PARA UNA NIÑA NEGRA

i.

We make love in his first language;
he teaches only in his second language:
What else is a puertorriqueño to do?

As he sings Colombian jazz songs, he beats
a rhythm on my buttocks, my back, my belly.
I catch words—*papeles, amor, revolución.*

I ask for her story, *"Las Flores para
una Niña Negra."* In *español* and *ingles*
he whispers the story in my ear:

*Una niña negra is hungry. It has
swallowed her until only her eyes,
limpid brown, exist in her face.*

*Her mamá tells her to sleep, for in her dreams
her mamá will bring tortillas, hot and crisp,
plump grains of rice, red beans in a spicy sauce.*

*Una niña negra closes her eyes, sleeps.
When she awakes, her mamá gives
her las flores, flores muy bonito,*

*brilliant yellow and red flowers
from her garden.* We finish.
He kisses the swell of my earlobe.

ii.

Between our sex scenes he quotes lines
from movies, *B* movies I have never seen.
He laughs because I believe his words.

He considers my admissions of naïveté
a challenge. He smiles before working
me up politically: *Can't you tell*

the difference between Reagan and Marx?
I know only *Masterplots*. He sighs.
He can no longer watch the movies.

The images are all translucent, and no amount
of complaining to theater owners seems to change
them. The other images he knows are real;

With care, a twelve-year-old boy balances
a small white box on his head,
as younger brothers and sisters,

the survivors, skip through the thin dust,
moving in single file towards the cemetery.
No adults walk with them.

Too many have been lost to hunger
and disease for this one to earn parents
an hour off from the sugar cane plantation.

Children bury children too small to labor
in the fields. In time they will learn
to grieve quickly, get on with living.

My lover says he will be a Marxist
until oppressed people no longer exist.
He kisses me full on the mouth.

GENESIS COLLAGE

What you wanted to be; what scared you most;
and the figure opposite of yourself.
— Erica Hunt

i.

Born raw
dark cloth.
Exhale
the truth—
Something horrible
cuts grandly,
terror.

Minutes
went slow.
I knew you,
them.

Silence;
velvet lining.

ii.

A star map,
no frame of reference.
Traveler/researcher
watching through
one-way glass.

Reactions—
My voice began
to rise
and crack.

　　　　　Demetrice Anntía Worley

Broke open,
wet.

iii.

In the cathedral,
lights went on.
Dazzled by liberty,
I learned
to embrace
the edge.

iv.

No reflections;
no shadows.
I loved
you all—

abortions,
births.

4. TESTIFY

NO POSITION IS A POSITION

As girls we catch our breaths
when family, friends, teachers,
strangers say *no*; we hear
you can't, ugly, skinny/fat,
nasty, bitch; slide into a vacuum,
silence comes easily, comforting.

As women we long for love,
partners to fill spaces we've
purposely left open: hearts
waiting for completeness;
intellects waiting for challenges.
When partners, lovers,
and those others we sex
just for the fun of it, say *no*,
we silence our tongues, swallow
whole words until we feel full,
then we starve/gorge ourselves
with food/clothes/relationship drama
until we are in comas,
eyes open wide shut.

We women want change,
new spheres, power.
We silence our tongues,
fear political labels,
the *F* word, *feminism*,
hyphens do no better,
radical-, black-, eco-;
we search for more inclusion
without losing what separates
us—perhaps *womanist*.
In the end, we might as well

Demetrice Anntía Worley

speak for ourselves,
hold the positions
we want,
love ourselves
with wicked glee.

All our words/silences
demonstrate our politics—
our power is in choice.

This position is my position;
I name it with my voice.

AN AFRICAN AMERICAN WOMAN LEARNS TO WRAP *HIJAB*: A PANTOUM

Stand before a mirror,
    hold selected *hijab*,
rectangle cloth, 2 feet by 6 feet long,
    Muslim women's public pronouncement.

Hold selected *hijab*,
    finger soft fabric between fingers,
Muslim women's public pronouncement,
    drape forehead, crown, and neck.

Finger soft fabric between fingers,
    eyes open, conscious decision,
drape forehead, crown, and neck,
    push back feminist thoughts.

Eyes open, conscious decision,
    pinch cloth, tight, use index finger and thumb,
push back feminist thoughts.
    Pull long end across neck, up, over crown,

pinch cloth tight, use index finger and thumb,
    frame caramel face in fabric.
Pull long end across neck, up, over crown.
    ignore light in eyes,

frame caramel face in fabric.
    Carry cloth down side of head,
ignore fear in eyes,
    across neck, up, over crown, use one straight pin.

Demetrice Anntía Worley

Carry cloth down side of head,
    emotions, smolder in check,
across neck, up, over crown, use two straight pins,
    anchor loose end.

Emotions, smolder in check,
    standing before a mirror.
Anchor loose ends
    with rectangle cloth, 2 feet by 6 feet long.

A DECENT WOMAN

i.

In Egypt, no decent woman
exhibits a need to look
into a stranger's eyes,
to display more than her hands
or face embraced by *hijab*,
to walk along the streets alone,
to laugh showing her teeth,
to be heard above the traffic.

ii.

In Egypt, I lost my feminism
in the folds of my *hijab*:
I walked modestly
beside my companion,
body and head covered;
hid my smile demurely
behind my exposed hands;
never raised my eyes
above a man's chest;
never offered a whispered opinion
on Islam and women
above the traffic's clamor.

Demetrice Anntía Worley

DANCING IN THE DARK

At an English conference presentation,
77 people and I breathe molecules

from Julius Caesar's last dying breath.
This is the only connection between us.

I am in a herringbone tweed suit.
Gray and black crosshatch pattern confines

my hips, chest, back. Hair twisted,
tight coil, no loose ends escaping.

Small pearl earrings, one in each ear,
match the thin strand around my neck.

I present papers in white academia.
I match their foreign movements.

My jerky fox trot is invisible to them.
They see a waltz of standard diction.

"She speaks so well for a black woman."
One or two others like me,

dancing to a rhythm, they can't hear,
smile, nod, exchange partners.

I return home, shed herringbone layer,
run hands over warm caramel skin,

wide hips, small breasts, ashy knees.
Put my hair in thick braids.

Muddy Waters on the box.
Soul slow dances back into my body.

SOUVENIR SNAPSHOT

Something waits beneath it, the whole story
doesn't show.

— Andrew Wyeth

A Sinai Desert photograph:
a four-star General smiling,
surrounded by six AK-47-armed
soldiers, squinting, in front
of a right-fender-dented,
green army truck, and
me, standing off to the left,
my caramel face floating
in yellow *hijab*, tanned hands
clenched by my sides.

CULTURAL WEAVING SKILLS

At the Oriental Carpet School,
another name for a child labor carpet factory,
in response to questions about the children's ages,
6 to 12 year olds,
the number of children working,
20 to 25 per room in a 100 rooms,
the number of hours they worked,
10 to 12 hours a day,
the amount they were paid,
1 Egyptian Pound ($0.17) per day,
and how much education they received,
no formal education, only carpet weaving skills,
to create one silk rug in a year's time,
that would sell for $20,000,
the shopkeeper looks at my *hijab*,
asks my opinion of Egypt.
Do you like pig meat?
I answer in my mind.
Afraid to offend him, I look at his feet;
I smile, behind my hand,
an attempt to make amends.

MY BODY IS IN FRAGMENTS

*When a butterfly flutters its wings in one part of
the world, it can eventually cause a hurricane in
another . . . .*

— Edward Lorenz

My face is more than one face; my body is in fragments—
an empty eye socket holds fires; two braids, coarse black
strands, rest on taut skin, protruding shoulder blades;
hands grasp lightning.

My face is more than one face; my body is in fragments—
ecru ear, seashell curl, turned to the ground; dirt-bleached
femur surrounds protruding rib cage; white-clay hand
prints pattern burnt sienna walls; feldspar idol's mouth
pursed/curved down, slack stone breasts hang waist high,
stone flesh surrounds clitoris.

My face is more than one face; my body is in fragments—
yellow eye-spots floating on a butterfly's flapping wings,
China's future storms in chaotic slumber; off the Galapagos,
a weak El Niño is invisible, warm waters weld, cold waters
sink; snow falls and falls and falls in Central Illinois.

My face is more than one face; my body is in fragments—
blue pebble mound rests on silica sand, spinning into black
silence.

Demetrice Anntía Worley

AMERICA DECLARES WAR ON GIRLS

Bright-eyed newscasters
  have long since given
    their cheery good nights
      when a low moan starts

deep in my throat—a ten-year-old
  boy calmly lines up his targets
    in the cross hairs: a girl's body
      tumbles into rough cedar chips,

her empty swing kisses its arc;
  another girl, laughs turns to touch
    her friend's arm, stumbles over her
      black and white sneakers, falls—

a vibration moves along my vocal
  cords, down my wind pipe—
    seventeen-year-old sweethearts
      push aside discarded cardboard,

partially eaten sandwiches, crumpled
  newspapers, making room for their
    two hour and thirty-seven minute old
      daughter before driving his dad's SUV

to the prom where friends wait
  eagerly to pose for a group picture—
    the moan fills my stomach, cramps
      my intestines; my legs shake—

a fourteen-year-old boy keeps
  vigil over a seven-year-old girl's
    stabbed body, hidden under his
      waterbed, he grunts a laugh

destroys one dimensional images
   of men/women over and over again,
      racking up thousands of video game
         points—the moan rises in my intestines

into my stomach, throat; I hear/feel
   myself screaming—a sixteen-year-old
      knocks a nine-year-old girl off her bicycle,
         pummels her with rocks. She stops moving.

He pulls her white cotton panties
   below her knees, jabs a stick into her vagina.
      She moans. He stuffs yellow/brown leaves
         in her mouth, stops her voice, her cries, her breath.

Demetrice Anntía Worley

A WOMAN'S OFFERING: A BOP

This January evening, Cairo is outside
my taxi window: stalled traffic,
people walking. Shop windows illuminate
women's long dresses, men's shoes,
a 12-year-old girl licking
the taxi's windshield.

The world is safe within their dreams.

This January evening in Cairo
a girl's pink tongue slowly slides,
leaving wet arcs on dusty glass.
The three men in the taxi, an Egyptian,
an Iraqi, and an American, ignore the girl,
drone on about the war. In the noisy street,
the girl's almond eyes ask questions American
dollars and Egyptian pounds cannot answer.

The world is safe within their dreams.

This January evening in Cairo
my brown eyes, surrounded by *hijab*,
never leave the girl's face. I offer folded hands
in prayer, *Enshallah*. She nods, presses
her small lips against my window;
seals our transaction with a kiss.

The world is safe within their dreams.

NOTES

"Tongues in My Mouth"

- *Tuwa wasteicillia maka kin lecela tehan yunkelo*: Whoever considers themselves beautiful, on earth, only endures.

- *Sa koon ain je gun*: Bright-white-flamed-instrument.

- *Ewúro ò fi tojo korò*: The bitter-leaf did not become bitter as a result of cowardice. (One does what one must, regardless of the actions or wishes of others.)

"Visual Markers"

- *The purpose of [the control unit] is to control revolutionary attitudes in the prison system and in society at large*: "Women's Control Unit: Marianna, FL." Women's Lives: Multicultural Perspectives. Gwyn Kirk and Margo Okazawa-Rey, eds. (Mayfield, 1998).

- The U.S. Federal Bureau of Prisons (BOP) High Security Unit (HSU) at the women's federal correctional institution in Lexington, Kentucky, which opened in October 1986, was closed in August 1988, through the efforts of prison activist groups and other concerned groups.

- **Alejandrina Torres** was granted clemency in September 1999 by President William J. Clinton.

- **Susan Rosenberg** was granted clemency in December 2000 by President William J. Clinton.

- **Silvia Baraldini** was repatriated to Italy in 1999 to serve the remainder of her sentence.

- **Assata Shakur** was sentenced to life in prison in 1973 for the death of a New Jersey State Trooper. In 1979 she escaped from prison. Shakur's whereabouts were unknown until she published her first book, *Assata Shakur: An Autobiography* (1987) in Cuba where she was granted political asylum.

"Femicide/*Femicidio* ~ The Murdered and Disappeared Women of *Ciudad Juárez*, México"

Sonnet *i*. Speaker: Señora Josephina Sanchez Cruz, Solana's and Isabel's mother.

- **eve of the dead**: November 1st. The night before November 2nd, All Souls Day. In Western Christianity, All Souls Day is a celebration of general intercession for the souls of the departed to reach heaven.

- *Virgen de Guadalupe*: The Virgin of Guadalupe (also Our Lady of Guadalupe) is a 16th century Roman Catholic Mexican icon that is said to represent an apparition of the Virgin Mary.

- *Ciudad Juárez*: Juárez City, México, is located across the border from El Paso, Texas. Its location makes an ideal site for assembly plants that make products which are sold in the United States of America as a result of the North American Free Trade Association (NAFTA). Since 1993 over 400 women have been murdered and over 5,000 women/girls have disappeared from Ciudad Juárez. Many of these women/girls worked at the factory/assembly plants.

Sonnet *ii*. Speaker: Isabel Sanchez Cruz, Solana's sister.

- *quinceañera*: fifteenth birthday celebration that marks passage from girlhood to womanhood.

- *Colonía Paz*: Peace Town. This composite shanty town represents the shanty towns on the outskirts of Ciudad Juárez where many of the women/girls live who work in the factory/assembly plants.

Sonnet *iii*. Speaker: Eva Flores Moreno, Solana's best friend and co-worker at the factory.

- *de la maquila*: of the assembly plant. *Maquila* is the shortened form of *maquiladora*, a factory/assembly plant which moved from the U.S. to Mexico where it takes in imported raw materials and produces goods for export to the U.S.

- *las chicas*: the girls

- *la muerta*: the dead

- *la frontera*: "the border" between the United States of and Mexico.

Sonnet *iv*. Speaker: Monica Campbell is a California native who has worked as a freelance journalist based in Mexico City since 2003. She has covered immigration, economic, and political topics including the murdered and missing women of Ciudad Juárez.

- **Found Sonnet**: All the text in this "found" sonnet, except the text inside the brackets, is taken from Monica Campbell's essay "Rethinking NAFTA" which appears on the PBS P.O.V. *Señorita Extraviada* "Maquiladora" Web page.

- **NAFTA**: The North American Free Trade Agreement is a trilateral trade bloc in North America created by the governments of the United States, Canada, and Mexico signed by the leaders of each country on December 17, 1992.

Sonnet *v*. Speaker: Dr. Irma Rodriguez. Dr. Rodriguez is a forensic specialist and was a state police commander. Her 17-year-old daughter, Paloma Villa, was killed in 2002 by unknown assailants.

• *caso de m'hija*: my daughter's case

• **pink/black crosses**: Groups such as *Mujeres por Juárez* (Women for Juárez), *Voces Sin Eco* (Voices without Sound/ Echo) and other volunteers paint a black and pink cross each time another woman is killed in Juárez. Hundreds of such crosses appear throughout Juárez.

Sonnet *vi*. Speaker: Women of Juárez. This group is a composite of the following groups who protest the police department's and the Mexican government's lack of action on solving the murders and disappearance of women and girls from Juárez: *Mujeres por Juárez* (Women for Juárez), *Voces Sin Eco* (Voices without Sound/Echo), and other volunteer groups.

• *ninas y mujeres*: girls and women

• *matadas*: killed (women)

• **Laura Ramos Monarrez, . . . Guadalupe Estrada Salas**: These names are those of actual murdered women from Juárez.

• *hijas y hermanas*: daughters and sisters

• *las policías*: the police

Demetrice Anntía Worley

- *mujeres del fugitive*: runaways (women)

- *el secreto*: the secret

- *evidencia destruida*: destroyed evidence

Sonnet *vii.* Speaker: A Black Woman Poet in Peoria Protests after Seeing Lourdes Portillos' Film Señorita Extraviada

- **Brach's candy corn:** The Brach company once made candy in the U.S. Its candy corn is now made in Mexico.

- **Six Local Black Women Murdered, . . . in Rural Countryside:** Between March 2001 and November 2004, the bodies of six African American women, who all were in their late thirties and in their forties, were discovered in rural Peoria, Tazewell, and Woodford counties in Illinois. With the discovery of the sixth African American woman's body, the Peoria Police Department was forced by Peoria churches and protests groups to increase their investigations into the women's deaths and to acknowledge that four additional African American women were missing.

In November 2004, Peoria County law enforcement did not believe that the six murdered Black women who had "'questionable lifestyles'... prostitutes or drug users" were killed by one person.

In January 2005 Larry Bright was arrested by the Peoria Police, and he confessed to killing eight African American women: in 2003, Sabrina Payne; in 2004, Barbara Williams, Linda K. Neal, Brenda Erving, Shaconda Thomas, Shirley Ann Trapp, Tamara Walls, and Laura Lollar.

On May 30, 2006, Larry Bright was convicted of seven counts of first degree murder and one count of drug-induced homicide. He was sentenced to seven consecutive life sentences plus 30 years in prison.

- **Wanda Jackson** is an African American woman believed, by many people in Peoria, to have been killed by serial killer Larry Bright.

SPECIAL THANKS

The poems in this book took over a decade to gain voice and to come together in one place. However, they were never alone. Many people along the way shared their love and constructive criticism with me as these poems came into being, to whom I give *love* and *thanks*, and to whom I offer *peace*: Mourning Clothes" is for Bessie Grayson; "Terra Firma" is for Henry Wilson; "Femicide/*Femicidio* ~ The Murdered and Disappeared Women of *Ciudad Juárez*, México" is for the over 400 to over 5,000 murdered and disappeared women and girls from *Ciudad Juárez*, Mexico; "Milk Teeth" is for Thomas Daniel Worley, Jr.; "Ten Words Liberate a Life" is for Ernestine Randle Worley; "Planting Shirt" is for DeLoris Edwards; for all of the names that do not appear below, you know who you are, I love/loved you dearly: Every creative writing course I took and every creative writing instructor I had at Bradley University, University of Illinois (Urbana), and Illinois State University, for helping me hone my craft; the institutional support from Bradley University which allowed me the time to revise a group of poems into a manuscript; my mentor and dear friend, you know who you are, for your keen insight and for helping me change a wobbly manuscript into this book; the Cave Canem Foundation (CC), "a home for the many voices of African American poetry and [who] is committed to cultivating the artistic and professional growth of African American poets," for selecting me as a Fellow before I learned, in three summer one-week retreats, that first and foremost, *I am a poet*; the 2004, 2005, and 2006 CC Summer Retreat Workshop Leaders and Fellows, for their poetic love, tears, support, criticism, and encouragement; Lita Hooper and Renee Simms for being my grrrls and sistah-artists; Niki Herd for holding my hand as I travelled on the path, for closely reading the "insides" with sharp eyes, and for being my grrrl and sistah-poet; Antoinette Brim, my grrrl, my sistah-poet separated from me at birth, for our friendship which nourishes me when I am too tired to move, consoles me in the silent black void, and makes me laugh when I think nothing can ever tickle me out of grief's icy grip; CC's "Good Brothah-men," you know who you are, for your support; M. Scott Douglass, for being an extraordinary editor, your publishing knowledge is cool refreshing water in a deep, deep well; Rachel Eliza Griffiths, my sistah-photographer/ sistah-poet, for gracing this book with her cover art; Kwame Dawes, my Brothah-poet, for writing a stunning foreword for this book, you put out the call "Forward," and I am responding, "Yeah man. One love"; Kevin Stein, my dear friend and Illinois Poet Laureate, for mentoring me for over 22 years and for believing in my voice; Stacey Robertson and Francesca Ammer, my dear-dear friends, for loving me during the last 16 years and 20 years, respectively, when I was whole and when I was broken; Timothy Daniel Worley and Michael D. Worley, my brothers, for forgiving me for being such a meany when we were young, and for being the best "little-big" brothers a "big" sister could ever want; Philomena Worley, my step–mother, Austin and Justin, my twin brothers, and Tanya Worley, my sister-in-law, for your warm loving hearts and arms; Thomas D. Worley, Jr., my father, for teaching me to see and trust my inner light and for helping me learn my life lessons; Ernestine Randle Worley, my mother, who taught me to talk the talk and to walk the walk, and who helped me learn what it means to be a strong Black woman; and especially to Charley Mabry, my laughing sunshine, for finding me in your own backyard, you will never have to search for me again—you are so right, I am worthy of every good thing that comes into my life—you are my joy, my happiness, and my love.

Demetrice Anntía Worley